TRADING OPTIONS ON TECH STOCKS:
SELLING PUTS & CALLS

Real Examples to Generate
Consistent Option Income and more

The INCOME INVESTING FOR INDIVIDUALS Series

ALAN KERRMAN

Trading Options on Tech Stocks
Copyright © 2015 Alan Kerrman, Notable Media. All rights reserved worldwide.

Copyright, Legal Notice, and Financial Disclaimer:

Thank you for supporting my work.
First Edition, v. 1.2
Published by NOTABLE MEDIA

ISBN-13: 978-1533368157

ISBN-10: 1533368155

To my sweetheart and our daughter: Thanks for giving me the time, space, and encouragement to write.

Also by Alan Kerrman:

Investing in DRIPs

(also available in audiobook format)

The Seven Step Rocket Start-Up Plan

Contents

Preface

Selling Options on Tech Stocks is One of the Best Ways to Regularly Take Money Out of the Market

As an individual investor who has finally realized that there is no HOLY GRAIL to tech investing, I'm intrigued by options premium and volatility. It's reassuring for me to know that there are great ways to take money out of the market on a regular basis, and that's what I've included here. Right up there with the power of dividend stocks, selling options on tech stocks (covered calls, cash-secured puts, and credit spreads) always feels like a smart way to leverage my investments in ways that the institutional traders can.

Those old trader sayings tell us: "be the casino, not the gambler"... or "be the landlord, not the tenant..." That's the power of selling options. Turn your investments into an option-selling income generator. But if you prefer to keep your technology stocks, you can use regular options sales to reduce your cost basis, eventually even creating holdings that have been fully paid for.

Here's a short, actionable book by an individual investor for other individual investors -- showing some real examples from current option prices. These are NOT trade ideas, but rather strategies for you to apply to your technology stock and options trading research.

Introduction

Thank you so much for reading my latest book: **Trading Options on Tech Stocks: Selling Puts & Calls** (Real Examples to Generate Options Income and more)!

Individual investors need to stick together, and we need to share actionable information. That's why I wrote my recent book on *Dividend Reinvestment Plans (DRIPs)*, and that's why I'm writing this options book. I want to share the kind of things I think about with my own personal, self-directed investing. I learned these strategies -- not to become rich -- but to support my family well, plan for retirement, create streams of income, and pay off our home and any debts.

It's easy to write a book like this because it's downright fun for me to talk about this stuff. Seriously, these are two of my favorite things: tech stocks and options! If we met on the street, at a cocktail party, or some other event or function, and started discussing my interest in finance and trading, these are the kinds of things I would share with you. And since I'm NOT a financial professional, I get to be completely honest, irreverent, contradictory, and downright open about what I feel.

I wrote this book to share with you ways I use options -- six primary trading strategies -- specifically applied towards technology growth and income stocks. There are other ways of course -- some simpler, some more advanced -- but this is how I trade options, and how I make money with options, so I'm happy to share with you what I do.

So here it is, my truth:

1. The finance professionals are out to get us [well, okay... maybe not all of them, but a heck-of-a-lot of them!]. We're just sheep to them, and the less we know, the more money they make. Fight back, people -- armed with knowledge, and skills in the financial markets.

2. The annual fees that even simple mutual funds take from your work 401K (or 403b) retirement accounts should drive you completely batty! It makes me crazy! I don't mind spending money, but I should get more 'upside' for my added fees/risk. Some of these managers consistently trail index funds - which means we pay for "management," but they can't even match their market benchmark indexes. Not saying it's easy, but these ridiculous fees don't help us.

3. We're supposed to think that all of this finance/ trading/investment stuff is way too hard to comprehend, but it's not. Sure there's a learning curve, but anything this

important is worth learning. Most people spend more time looking at restaurant menus, planning vacations, or shopping for a car... Not us!

4. I know too many people who have let real money slip through their fingers, and the trick to not letting that happen again is to be more informed, and always continue to learn. (Me included!)

5. Buying options -- which erode and expire -- is something I pretty much stopped doing (unless it's a vertical or calendar spread trade), because selling options makes you the *bank*, and not the *customer*, or the *casino* and not the *gambler*, etc. What this means is that most of my trading strategies her involve selling options, often getting paid the moment you put on the trade.

6. Making smaller wins over and over again for retail traders is often a better plan than expecting your favorite stock to double, triple, or quadruple. Besides, if your stock doubles, would you immediately sell it and lock in those big gains, or would you hang on to see if it's potentially going higher? If it doesn't pay a dividend, and you don't regularly sell options against your holdings, it's possible to hold big winners for a long time and get zero benefit from them. And the web is filled with stories of people who 'held on' while their stock went all the way up to the sky, and came all the way back down, perhaps even below their original purchase price. *Ouch.* I'll take a string of singles, doubles, and triples any day, rather than pray for home runs, or grand slams. (Okay, no more baseball analogies.)

So that's what this book is: a collection of useful options strategies that I regularly use, that I think about constantly, and that I practice and refine. They are applied based on overall market conditions, underlying stock activity (relation to 52-week high/low, volatility, etc), time decay, cost-basis reduction, return-on-risk, and more.)

I'm not selling anything here -- except for this book obviously, that cost you less than a *Chai Tea Latte* at Starbucks! [I get to share what I know - which is fun, and you can tell your friends to buy my book if you want -- or leave a review if you want, to help some other nice strangers find it.] I have no course for you to buy, no membership sites, no software tools for sale. I don't want to manage your money -- I'm not a registered investment advisor anyways, and I don't manage anyone else's assets. I'm just an individual investor -- with a full-time job outside of finance -- making serious headway with our personal finances, wealth building, and long-term retirement planning. Learn with me!

This book is filled with my personal perspectives on option trade strategies related specifically to technology stocks -- but please understand this statement clearly: the specific strategies and examples in this book are NOT trade ideas. Nothing that you read here is for anything more than informational, educational, and entertainment value. I use real tech companies, with their real stock tickers, and mention the real value of their real underlying options, but only so you can see how I think about this stuff, how it works, and what to look for. How I put on these trades -- that's the reason I use real prices and real stocks. Think about these as tools and as open-ended strategies only...

This book is also NOT intended to be an absolute beginner's guide to options. I'm sure there are many other fantastic choices you can grab if that's what you need. (I've read a bunch of those books myself!) But that said, I think this material is pretty straightforward and relatively easy-to-understand, so beginners are very much welcome here. It does get easier each time you dig into these options strategies.

And finally...

I hope this short book gets you excited about the possibilities of trading and investing with options. And I want you to see specifically how to trade PUTS and CALLS around your favorite **technology stocks** to create income, reduce risk, and lower your overall costs of investing. Derivatives -- products like options that 'derive' value based on other products -- are only dangerous if used in haphazard ways. I'll show you examples here of how I take LESS risk overall because of my options trading.

Now let's talk about some 'best practices' and trader habits from my perspective...

1. Our Trading Habits

I had a friend tell me that every single time -- absolutely 100% of the time -- he bought a stock, ETF, or mutual fund, it immediately went down in price. Even if eventually it went up over a longer period, he was always instantly bothered by those intra-day fluctuations in price.

I was sympathetic and empathetic with that feeling of choosing poorly, but I would always ask him, "why did you buy that stock now?" It was always a story about an industry, tech, growth possibility, or other 'anecdotal evidence'... (With him, it was never charts, fundamentals, or volatility.)

Once you start watching the markets even a little bit, you'll realize that even though it's quite difficult (or for some, downright impossible) to accurately "time" the market when you buy stocks -- especially technology stocks, there are three common ways to think about this whole process of managing our own investments.

This is why most traders -- and investors -- fall into these three camps:

1. Chartists & Market Analysts

Analyzing Chart Patterns: Those who watch stock charts, looking for support and resistance levels, moving averages, trends, and recognizable chart patterns. These can be tracked with candlestick charts, simple line charts, or point and figure charts -- all with or without trading volume -- to give the trader/investor some level of information about what has been going on over various time frames. 'Chartists' draw trend lines and use any number of overlays and indicators including Fibonacci retracements, stochastics, VWAP, MACD, RSI, Bollinger bands, Ichimoku clouds, and more. If you're interested in this kind of stock selection, then you'll constantly study patterns of support and resistance as well as price channels, reversals, flags/pennants, wedges, cup with handles, head and shoulders patterns, and more. Japanese candlestick charting is also a common tool with market 'technicians' who look for the engulfing patterns, the doji, harami, abandoned baby, dark cloud cover, and more. (*I like this stuff!*)

2. Value Investors & Fundamentalists

Researching Fundamentals: There are those investors (and some traders) who are only clearly interested in buying stocks whose underlying business value makes solid financial sense. Fundamental investors look at market cap, price to earnings (P/E and forward P/E), price/sales, PEG, margins (gross, operating, and profit), debt, cash flow, and more. Of course, since there are so many ways to analyze this data, it's not as cut and dry as it seems. It's the idea that if you buy a few shares of company stock -- assuming you had enough billions of dollars! --you would be comfortable enough in the underlying value of the business to buy the entire company. That takes research... and some amount of due diligence. (*I like this stuff, too!*)

3. Premium Sellers

Selling Volatility: The third way -- sadly ignored by many retail traders -- is to trade or invest based on some understanding of a stock's current implied and historic volatility. How much does your stock move around in price? Is it volatile, explosive? Does it regularly drop lower or scream higher, after earnings for example? Since volatility affects (increases) option prices, then option sellers (us!) want to use higher volatility to collect more option premium. The extra premium reduces our risk and can become essentially a *margin of error* -- for our trades. If you want to buy 100 shares of a tech stock like Adobe Systems Inc (ticker: ADBE), its options pay more now because of higher volatility (and its upcoming earnings), than a company like Cisco Systems (ticker: CSCO). The volatility is simply a measure of how the price 'varies' or moves over time. (*I really like this stuff, too!*)

Some traders use more than one of these outlooks above, while many combine all three. It's also possible to have certain trades that are purely fundamental (certain swing trades, income investing (puts spreads), or buy/hold long term ownership), purely chart-driven (swing/day trades, condors, spreads, etc), and those based on volatility (selling premium and/or time decay; lowering cost basis, etc).

I also vary my approach based on which account I'm trading. I think it's reasonable to not only diversify your holdings -- which Wall Street regularly tells us to do -- but it's also fine to diversify your trading strategies. That's why I use stocks/ETFs, dividend reinvestment plans, all manner of options trading, and index and commodity futures in my taxable trading accounts, as well as mutual funds and index funds in my long-time tax-deferred (401k/403b) retirement accounts.

My Trading Routine

So let's talk about developing a set of tools that prepares you to buy and sell in the US equity, options, and futures markets. I regularly watch the E-mini S&P, Dow, and Nasdaq futures (symbol: /ES, /YM, and /NQ) to give me an overall sense of the market from any point starting Sunday evening until Friday's close. I also watch overall market volatility with /VX, VIX, and others, as well as some commodity indicators (oil, gold, USD, EUR, etc), and always maintain watch lists of my favorite stocks, and any new ideas. We'll talk about ways to get new ideas later -- crowd-sourcing and stock screeners -- but I believe that trading the same underlying stocks over and over again is a good way to get to know the cycles of the market and become more consistent with earnings.

I also keep paper, and spreadsheet-based, trade journals to track my progress. I have modest monthly goals for my account, and tracking them is the only way I know if I'm making real progress. It always keeps me calm and focused when I trade to know that I will be writing down the details of my trades. It's an extra step I've taken towards becoming more deliberate with my investing and trading. I use the notebook to make quick comments about my entry/exit, targets, support, and the overall market conditions, while the spreadsheet helps me track my profit/loss returns over a longer period.

But let's discuss financial goals, because it helps to be as specific as you can. For example, if you're trading a $30,000 account, and it's your goal to earn at least 10% for the year, then $3000 over 12 months only requires a gain of $250 per month (or $62.50/week over four weeks). With options, that can sometimes be accomplished with defined risk trades while the rest of the portfolio 'enhances' your return.

What if I want more than that?

If you want to earn more than that, start with a more modest annual goal, break it down monthly, and try first to meet that each month. After consistently meeting that goal for at least three months, for example, then simply adjust your goal based on your actual results. If you have a $30,000 account as above, and you're easily making about $600 a month, that would net you $7200 per year in gains, or a return of 24%. It's just not reasonable to assume that you can consistently earn that much on your trading account unless you have already organized your trading, systematized your tracking, and proved your performance to yourself over time. But once you do, that can be your new performance goal for tracking.

It's also likely that as your account size gets larger, it's both easier and harder to generate a bigger return. It's easier because you have more capital so you can be involved in more trades, but it's harder because those trades that lose money have to lose less than your winning trades must gain. Tracking this, plus trading discipline will make sure you grow no matter what your account balance.

So if you're regularly trading $100,000+, you're goals might start off at a more modest 5-8%, far greater than any bank would give you in money market, CD, or savings interest. That 8% or $8000 goal, is about $667 per month, or $167 per week. If you're trading options primarily, then calculate your maximum risk per trade (for defined or undefined risk), and decide how many trades you need monthly to reach your goal. (You may decide for example that you will not risk more than $250-500 on any single trade, even with a $100,000 account.) (This is why I also trade futures and futures options, and invest in dividend stocks, because each trade win, options premium, or dividend payment gets me closer to my overall monthly goals.)

So now let's talk about a few tools I use daily, or at least a few times per week...

2. My Trader & Investor Secret Weapons

The days of getting your trading ideas from random strangers, your barber/dentist, or your brother-in-law are clearly over. Over! Retail investors also have to realize that if they hear about a company on the evening news, NPR, or in the newspaper, then it's very likely that the 'value' or 'growth' concept that was reported on is already completely baked into the current price of the stock. Remember everyone likely heard the same news stories that you did -- and possibly even three months earlier.

But the real edge now is technology, crowd-sourcing, and tools that most people don't use. I like real up-to-date tech tools, with a little bit of crowd-sourced information. But no, I don't like those regular 'chat rooms' about stocks. Why? Because many of the "bulls" of a particular stock are already holding shares, possibly underwater, and will sell immediately if they can help generate enough positive interest in their holdings. This style of 'pump & dump' is everywhere -- so be on the lookout.

Hopefully, you already know about all of these tools and resources below, and use them regularly. But if not, you must check them out before you invest any more funds in the market. I consider them my 'secret' weapons, even though they're not mine, and they're all freely available to anyone... They've changed my world!

FINVIZ

For a quick visual glance at the entire stock market, I love the website FinViz.com, which is short for financial visualizations. When you first visit the site, you'll see all sorts of useful information on their homepage about the current market. It's a quick way to see a snapshot of the Dow, Nasdaq, and S&P intraday charts, along with advancing/declining stocks, new highs/new lows, and the SMA50/200, and a bull/bear indicator.

Below the market information, their screener shows a quick list of some ticker symbols that are the top gainers/ losers of the day, with new highs/new lows, unusual volume, and more. They even have a screened list that identifies stocks by some specific charting signals: trend line support and resistance, double tops and bottoms, and well as rising and falling triangles, wedges, and channels.

But to me, the two most powerful tools at this site are the heat maps and their screener. (The heat map is in the right column on the home page, or under their maps tab.)

You can see stocks (red to green) that represent a sliding scale of down 3%, flat and up 3%. The brighter the red, the bigger the down percentage, and the brighter the green, the more the stock is up. To prevent traders/investors from chasing after low-priced stocks that have spiked or plummeted, the size of the box represents market cap of the stock. Each visualizer is also well organized by sector. With their ticker search, you can find stocks on the heat map to see how their industry, sector, and competitors are doing in the same period.

The FINVIZ heat-map defaults at S&P 500 showing '1 Day Performance,' but their drop-down menu shows how powerful this is. You can also see the entire world's markets or the full list of stocks traded on US exchanges -- not just the S&P. Their ETF visualizer can quickly show you what sectors are working, and how the inverse ETFs fare in comparison.

Their daily, weekly, monthly, 3-month, 6-month, 1-year, and YTD heat-map settings are also very robust. Do you want to see how well your sector's stocks are doing compared to each other? As I'm writing this, Qualcomm (ticker: QCOM) is down -7.89% year-to-date, while Harris Corp (ticker: HRS) is up +10.83% YTD. Comparing these two stocks in the tech sector -- communications equipment, both with dividend yields over 2%, could be useful when selling options on a new position.

When you double-click on a stock, you're brought to a detail page with daily, weekly, and monthly charts and lots of company and financial data, including P/E, EPS, debt, margins, insider ownership percentage, performance, beta, and more.

They also have a 'bubble' version of their visualizer that is also useful for finding new stocks to add to your watch lists.

Plus, their stock screener is downright amazing -- just go try it! Choose technology sector, 'optionable,' and then any other filters you want, and then sort the columns. Powerful stuff.

Finviz has a paid plan (about $300/year or $40/month as of this writing), but I've only ever used their free tools. Their paid Elite plan adds the functionality of real-time quotes, pre-market data, more advanced charting, back testing, and other benefits. HIGHLY RECOMMENDED.

STOCKTWITS

If you're looking for a constant stream of good trading ideas, commentary, some noise, and charts, then it makes sense to join StockTwits.com. Essentially it's a Twitter application that helps you crowd-source your trading ideas on a single platform because all stock symbols are tagged with the "$". I think it's a great way to know what stocks people are 'talking' about, and by extension, which stocks are 'trending' in terms of social interaction.

They have a social signals heat map that shows trending ticker symbols that can be set at one, six, twelve, or 24 hours. Combine that with their social tracking charts ('Unusual Social Volume'), and you will know what stocks and industries are peaking in discussions. These social spikes are likely from news events, being heavily watched, discussed, and traded over the same 1D, 7D, 30D, or 90D.

On a recent visit, I found that messages about big data analysis software company Splunk, Inc (ticker symbol: SPLK) had recently risen 1150%. I then added the stock to my watch list. It can be the best way to find out about trending, moving, volatile, or news-worthy stocks.

The power of Stocktwits is the ability to 'follow' those traders and investors whose ideas make sense to you, thereby controlling the information that you see. You can also follow your favorite stocks and see the discussions, charts, commentary, and trades of that stock by anyone on the platform. And each stock page shows the latest message stream, the price chart (1d, 1w, 1m, 3m, 6m, 1y, and all), as well as charts of the volume of recent messages, and a rolling 7-day basis bullish/bearish sentiment chart. HIGHLY RECOMMENDED.

TASTYTRADE

If you search YouTube for options trading videos, you've likely seen hundreds of great options and trading videos from the (newish) financial network TastyTrade.com. It was started by trader/CEO Tom Sosnoff, a former CME options market-maker and co-founder of Thinkorswim (which sold to TD Ameritrade in 2009). If you watch the network live during the day on the web, you'll see a number of different shows featuring veteran traders (Tom Sosnoff, Tony Battista, Ask Slim, Liz & Jenny, ShadowTrader Uncovered, and others), new trader coaching, market commentary, great research segments on trading, options math, an entrepreneurial bootstrap segment, futures discussion, call-in segments, discussions about sports and food, and more. It's funny, irreverent, informative, inspiring, empowering, and more. Open the show archives - categorized for beginning, intermediate, and advanced traders -- and dive in if you're curious, you'll be very glad that you did! HIGHLY RECOMMENDED.

DOUGH

Dough is an options trading tool created by the team at TastyTrade. It gives traders the ability to visualize options trades, standard deviations, probabilities, and more. The app, which integrates with ThinkorSwim accounts from TD Ameritrade (I seriously refer you to T.O.S. above all others brokers! http://bit.ly/TDameritradeOPTIONS), also allows stocks and options trading, access to the Tastytrade videos and live stream, as well as a chance to follow the trades of a number of options traders connected to their company and financial network. It's a powerful app, even in demo mode, and it works great on my iPad. The visual representations of risk profiles, standard deviation, break-even points, and more will make even the most complex options strategy seem very clear. HIGHLY RECOMMENDED.

BONUS

Let me add to the resources above by saying that I subscribe to some free email lists: BarChart, barchart.com, has a nice morning snapshot email called "Morning Call." It's free, and it gives a quick summary of overnight markets and news, U.S. stock preview, market commentary, upgrades and downgrades, and a global event calendar. I read some stuff at seekingalpha.com, and stay current with bigger trends in business, technology, and entrepreneurship over at medium.com. (Of course, Yahoo

Finance and Google Finance are also great stops during your morning routine!)

I also use an app on my iPad called StockTouch from Visible Market over at stocktouch.com, available from the iTunes app store. It has a very powerful free version, but also has a real-time premium feature for $20 a year, which I'm planning on trying soon. I've made my own heat-map watch lists there, and it's another very quick and powerful way to see the market. It can show maps based on price changes, volume, change relative to S&P500, vs sector, P/E ratio, and dividend yield.

Lastly, I have started consistently using a trading journal. It helps me stay true to my own 'trading rules' and strategies, and also lets me note the market conditions at the time of my trades. I found a good one to use with stocks, options, and futures from incrediblyusefulnotebooks.com. HIGHLY RECOMMENDED.

Now let's take a top-down view on the entire technology sector before we look at trading it.

3. Technology Stocks & ETFs

What are so many investors attracted to technology stocks? Well, that's an easy one. What does fiber optics, cell phones, personal computers, nanorobots, satellite communications, solar cells, the internet, transistors and microchips, and 3D printing have in common? Growth.

Tech stocks are pretty common and well-known companies for investors because they are often the most high-growth industry leaders, society's innovators, and true media darlings. Stocks of companies like Apple, Google, Microsoft, Intel, VMware, Facebook, First Solar, Twitter, and others have also made small fortunes for many individual traders and investors across the globe.

As you likely already know, the technology sector is pretty massive and includes electronics, information technology, and many growth industries. It also filters through our entire economy. Apple Inc (ticker symbol: AAPL) is actually in the *Consumer Goods* sector [the electronic equipment industry], although it's considered one of the most widely-known technology stocks. Tesla (ticker symbol: TSLA) is also in Consumer Goods sector [the auto manufacturers - major industry] although the electric car and battery technology is what drives many investors to buy the shares.

Do you consider any other stocks largely technology companies? What about other retailers, any conglomerates, or financial institutions? I do, and I don't think it matters as we track tech-related growth, trade our options and invest in these companies. Online you can find lists that describe the 32 separate industries that are in the technology sector:

Application software (companies like Adobe, Intuit, Red Hat, and Salesforce(.)com)

Business software & services (companies like Citrix Systems, Iron Mountain, Microsoft, and NetSuite)

Communication equipment (companies like Cisco Systems, Ciena Corp, Nokia Corporation, and Qualcomm)

Computer-based systems (companies like Acer, Cray, Hewlett-Packard, and Lenovo)

Computer peripherals (companies like Stratasys and 3D Systems)

Data Storage Devices (companies like EMC Corp, SanDisk, Seagate Technology, and Western Digital)

Diversified Communication Services (companies like Crown Castle, Level Three Communications, and Telecom Italia)

Diversified Electronics (companies like Mitsubishi Electric Corp, Corning Inc, and Kyocera Corp)

Healthcare Information Service (companies like WebMD Health Corp, athenahealth, inc, and Cerner Corporation)

Internet Information Providers (companies like Google, Baidu, and Facebook)

Internet Service Providers (companies like United Online, Spark Networks, and SMTP, Inc)

Internet Software & Services (companies like NetEase Inc, SINA Corporation, and Renren, Inc)

Long Distance Carriers (companies like General Communication and HC2 Holdings)

Multimedia & Graphics Software (companies like Konami Corp, Electronic Arts, and Electronic Arts, Inc.)

Networking & Communications Devices (companies like Cisco Systems, Palo Alto Networks, and Juniper Networks)

Personal Computers (companies like Apple, Hewlett-Packard, and Dell)

Printed Circuit Boards (companies like Jabil Circuit, Plexus Corp, and TTM Technologies)

Processing Systems & Products (companies like MSCI Inc, CoreLogic, and Plantronics, Inc)

Scientific & Technical Instruments (companies like Garmin, FLIR Systems, and Trimble Navigation)

Security Software & Services (companies like Symantec, Check Point Software, and Brady Corp)

Semiconductor - Broad Line (companies like Intel, Taiwan Semiconductor, and ARM Holdings)

Semiconductor - Integrated Circuits (companies like Broadcom, Analog Devices, and Marvell Technology Group)

Semiconductor - Specialized (companies like Altera Corp, NVIDIA Corporation, and First Solar, Inc)

Semiconductor Equipment & Materials (companies like Applied Materials, KLA-Tencor, and Synopsys, Inc)

Semiconductor - Memory Chips (companies like Micron Technology, Rambus, and Integrated Silicon Solution)

Technical & System Software (companies like SAP, Salesforce, and VMware)

Telecom Services - Domestic (companies like Verizon, AT&T, Chunghwa Telecom Co)

Telecom Services - Foreign (companies like Nippon Telegraph and Telephone, China Telecom, and Telef)

Wireless Communications (companies like Cellcom Israel, Brasil Telecom, America Movil SAB de CV)

Information & Delivery Services (companies like Broadridge, Dun & Bradstreet Corp, and Morningstar Inc)

Information Technology Services (companies like IBM, Wipro Ltd, and Accenture)

What about Exchange Traded Funds?

It's also possible to trade options on technology stocks using exchange traded funds, little baskets of stocks that act as a mutual fund but trade intraday like a stock. Just make sure your ETF choices are optionable -- not just for the sake of this material -- but also for your ability to hedge your purchases, reduce your overall costs, and trade around your core holdings. All of those ETF's listed below currently have options, and some also have weekly options.

There are already at least a few dozen ETFs that fall into the technology category and many have very narrow categories of stocks (specifically semiconductor stocks, cloud computing, social media, or cyber security, for example.) For our needs, we must also watch that these ETFs and their underlying options, have enough volume to warrant trading them.

XLK - Select Sector SPDR Trust Technology Select Index
VGT - Vanguard Info Tech Index
IYW - iShares US Technology ETF
SKYY - First Trust ISE Cloud Computing Index Fund ETF
SMH - Market Vectors ETF TR Semiconductor
XSD - SPDR S&P Semiconductor ETF
KWEB - KraneShares Trust CSI China Internet ETF
SOCL - Global X Funds FDS Social Media ETF

SSG ProShares Trust UltraShort Semiconductors
TECL - Direxion Shares Trust Technology Bull 3X Shares
TECS - Direxion Shares Technology Bear 3X Shares ETF
ROM - ProShares Ultra Technology
USD - ProShares Ultra Semiconductor
BIB - ProShares Ultra Nasdaq Biotechnology

You can also generally trade the Nasdaq index ETFs as a proxy for technology stocks:

QQQ - Powershares QQQ
QLD - ProShares Ultra QQQ
TQQQ - ProShares UltraPro QQQ

(Note: If you're bullish on tech you can always do contrary trades against a bearish ETF. Just always be very careful with the leveraged ETFs. Options contracts are already essentially leveraged!)

Opportunity Cost On Tech Stocks

Technology traders and growth and momentum traders, in general, usually don't want to miss out on fast-climbing stock price opportunity. This is the main reason that some traders/investors avoid many of the options strategies, and premium-generating trades outlined in this book.

No one wants to miss out. *What if I have a covered call on Tesla, and the stock goes to the moon? What if the*

shares of First Solar are ripping higher, but all I have is
bull put spreads?

The problem is that too many people are 'waiting' for that double, triple, or quadruple (2X, 3X, or 4X) move in their shares, but let's look at it from the other side.

If everyone you know bought Google at $400, do you want to buy it at $550? And what about those Google shareholders (ticker symbols: GOOG and GOOGL) who tell themselves that they will sell when the stock gets to $800? Who will buy the stock at $800? Sure, someone will -- if the company's growth, earnings, prospects, and perceived value are worth it at that point.

But since moves like that can take time, options income will reduce your cost basis while you trade around, and enter and exit your positions. If I bought GOOG here at $527.20, I'd take advantage of some options. The $570 CALL that expires in 67 days pays $480 bid. And the stock would have to be above $570 for it to get exercised. Hmmm.

So let's get started...

4. Strategy I

Selling Puts

Let's start with an example of a trade that I really like: selling a put option first instead of buying the shares outright. If I want to buy a stock right now at its current price, I'm interested in first finding out how much I can get paid to wait, and buy it later.

THE BASICS: Selling a put obviously means that at a specific price, I am obligated to buy 100 shares of the stock up until a specific expiration date. The concept is powerful because you get paid to buy (*potentially*) a stock cheaper than today's price. If the stock stays above your strike price to expiration, you keep the premium received and are not obligated to buy. If you're willing to buy a specific tech stock today -- with cash -- then would you buy it lower, and get paid a premium to wait?

OBJECTIONS:

The standard objection to selling a put with any growth stock is that you might miss out on the rocket ship! If you think the stock is definitely, and immediately, going higher, then you're only participation in the growth will be to collect the premium without ever owning the shares. However, what works well with volatile tech stocks is quantity. If you want to buy 500 shares of a certain stock, why not buy 300 shares now (with cash or margin), and sell two puts. If the stock goes up, you will participate in the move, and you'll keep the additional options premium. If the stock goes down, you may get a chance to buy the last 200 shares at a lower price, dollar-cost-averaging your position. Obviously if the stock price goes way down, both an outright purchase of 500 shares, or a hybrid 300 share purchase and the 2 put sales will lose money, but you will have a lower basis for recovery mode.

SAMPLE TECH TRADES:

Imagine that I currently like the social media stock Twitter, Inc [ticker symbol: TWTR], and that at $36.44 per share recently, and nearly flat year-to-date, I think it's a good buy right here. (Again remember that this is just a 'mind experiment' using real prices, none of these are trade recommendations!)

Sample trade:

So if I buy 100 shares of TWTR today on the open market at $36.44, it will cost me $3,644, plus transaction fees.

In case you're curious, most online brokers are in the $7 to $10 range, with a couple cheaper (IB is $1), and a few more expensive ($12-15 per transaction). I currently use

ThinkorSwim from TDAmeritrade [this link: http://bit.ly/TDameritradeOPTIONS], and pay in the $7 range, but I chose them not just because of price, but because I prefer their whole trading platform.

But if I agree to buy TWTR at $34 a share in 51 days, then I will get paid $70 today (minus fees) by selling a **TWTR JUL $34 PUT**.

If TWTR is below $34 at July expiration, I will have to pay $3400 (plus fees) to take delivery (exercise) of the stock.

But here's what I love about selling PUTS. If I was willing to buy this social media tech stock today for $3,644, wouldn't it be better to buy it at $3,400 in 51 days? And since I get paid $70 to wait, it would only cost $3400 - $70 (option premium) - fees (variable) = $3330.

So instead of $36.44 per share today, or $34 per share in July, my options premium received lowers my cost to $33.30, without fees. Even assuming high transaction fees ($10) and exercise fees ($20) with the various brokers, this transaction costs only $3,360 or $33.60 per share.

If I sold a closer strike price -- like the **TWTR JUL $35 PUT** -- also with 51 days-to-expiration (DTE), I'd collect $104 (minus fees), and be obligated to buy at or below $35 per share or $3500 - 104 + fees ($30) = $3,426 or $34.26 per share.

This means that even if the stock moves from today's price $36.44 all the way down to $34.26 in July, I am still at break-even! That's a drop of -5.98%, and that downside protection is a one of the best aspects of selling puts.

Because there are monthly options (third week), and many tech stocks also have monthly options, let's look at a shorter time-frame.

Imagine selling the **TWTR JUN $36 PUT** for the weekly option that expires in 30 days. At the time of this writing, with the stock at $36.44, that $36 PUT is an at-the-money (ATM) option because it's right here near the stock price. It pays $110 (minus fees), and would obligate us to buy 100 shares of Twitter at $3600 - $110 - fees = $3520 (assuming average $10 transaction and $20 exercise fees). That lets us buy TWTR in a month for $35.20 instead of today's price.

(We'll leave fees out from now on because they vary widely. But add or subtract whatever fees you want when you look at the examples that follow.)

VARIATIONS:

A good way to hedge your trading and investing is by always using a combination of selling puts and outright stock purchases. If you want 100 shares, consider an outright put sale. If you want 200 shares, buy 100 shares now, and sell one put contract for 30 to 60 days out. For 300, 500, or 1000 shares or more, choose a balance between premium selling and outright purchases. In a flat or bearish market, consider more puts than outright purchases. (You'll also see a related variation trade in the chapter on bull put spreads.)

Sample trade:

Assuming I'm interested in the cybersecurity solutions stock FireEye, Inc (ticker symbol: FEYE), I'll combine an outright purchase with some put sales for additional shares. Let's say I want to buy/obligate to buy a total of 400 shares.

Buy 100 shares of FEYE at $53.11 or $5,311, plus fees. Sell-to-open 3 FEYE $50 PUTs that expire in 17days at .65 credit each, or $65 for a total of $195, minus fees.

Is there risk? Yes, but less than owning 400 shares outright. Two things can happen here that I like: first the stock can continue to go higher, and I'll keep the $195 in put premium, show a gain on my 100 shares, which would have an adjusted basis of $5311-195= 5116, minus fees. If the stock pulls back to $50 in the next 17 days, I'll buy 300 shares cheaper than my first 100, which would now show a loss. The new shares would cost 300 x $50 - premium received ($195), or $14,805, minus fees, or $49.35 per share, compared to $53.11 for my first lot. The average basis on all 400 shares combined would now be $50.29, (without fees), a price I need to be comfortable with... (Then I could sell some covered calls.)

Now let's discuss another favorite strategy of mine.

5. Strategy II

Covered Calls

THE BASICS: A covered call is a call option sold against blocks of 100 shares of stock that you own. The sold call obligates you to sell at that specific price at or before the expiration date.

OBJECTIONS:

With tech growth stocks, many traders and investors are afraid to sell covered calls because they don't want to limit their upside potential. But it's common for these sold options to regularly expire in our favor, and then the overall cost of your holdings goes down when you consider the option premiums you've collected. It's also true that if your favorite technology company has no forecastable news, earnings calls, or scheduled conferences before expiration, then it might be totally clear to obligate the stock by selling calls.

SAMPLE TECH TRADES:

When I buy a stock outright, I consider it's covered call possibilities almost immediately. If I like the return at the time of purchase, I'll do a BUY-WRITE immediately, which is where you buy shares of a stock and simultaneously sell 1 call contract for each 100 shares. I do this because if the return works to be 'called away' or exercised, it's a win-win for me.

Either the stock gets called away and I make the full profit I saw when I entered the trade, or the growth tech stock stays flat and I keep the premium collected to lower my cost basis. Obviously, the key is to do this only on stocks you want to own.

Say I'm interested in data-storage solutions company SanDisk Corporation stock (ticker symbol: SNDK), recently trading at $63.77.

Sample trade:

Buy 100 shares of SNDK at $63.77 or $6377, plus fees.
Sell-to-Open (STO) 1 SNDK $66.5 CALL (39days to expiration) for 1.88, or $188, minus fees
Total cost: $6192 (without fees).

What I like about this trade is that I was already interested in SanDisk at these prices, and was willing to spend $6377 to buy it. With this covered call, the stock now costs me only $6192, with the added obligation to sell at $66.50 within 39 day, if the stock gets there. Since that's 4.28% higher in 39 days, I'd be happy to part with my shares if we get there. I can always repeat the trade later if I want.

But if I'm bullish about the stock, but doubt that it can reach $66.50 before my sold call expires, that premium could be mine to keep either way. It's a great way to change my basis from $63.77 to $61.92. What I'd want to watch for is company earnings dates, ex-dividend dates (SNDK pays a 1.80% yield annually), and any other news that might affect this stock during the covered call time period. There actually is a SNDK dividend that will be paid about a week after this option expires so it could get interesting! Either the stock moves and gets exercised by the option buyer to claim the dividend -- and we make our 4.28% in 39 days -- or the call expires in our favor and we earn the $0.30 per share dividend as well, another $30, reducing our overall cost even lower.

VARIATIONS:

One of these easiest ways to keep open the possibility of upside growth is to only cover some of your holdings. For example, if you have 200 shares, consider only selling one contract, obligating 100 shares and allowing the other 100 shares to freely move. If the call expires in your favor, the added premium lowers your basis for the 200 shares.

It's also possible to sell a disproportionate amount of calls to your holdings. If you own 500 shares and you're very bullish, but still want to take advantage of options premiums, you could sell one contract and leave 400 shares uncovered. In a neutral market where you still wanted to leave some stock open to upside movement, you could sell four contracts and leave 100 shares uncovered. As the options expire -- without exercise -- recalculate your cost basis because it might be possibly to sell a lower strike call in a flat or declining market.

For example:

Let's assume you bought 500 shares of stock in IT-storage hardware solutions company EMC Corp (ticker symbol: EMC) at $27.24 for a total cost of $13,620, plus commissions. To cover most of the shares, you decide to sell four $28 calls with 40 days to expiration at $0.52 or $52, taking in $208, minus commissions. If the 40-day options expires worthless, you would calculate your new basis by taking your original purchase price for all 500 shares, minus the options premium received on four contracts, and then divide by 500 for your new basis: $13,620 - $208 / 500 shares = $26.83 per share, as compared to $27.24. Next cycle, it's now safe for you to sell $27 calls at-the-money if the market conditions warrant it.

6. Strategy III

Bull Put Spreads

THE BASICS: A bull put spread (which is a credit spread) is the sale of a put with the simultaneous purchase of a lower strike put as a hedge. Because the put sold is closer to the actual price of the underlying it pays more. The purchased put below is further away from the strike, so it's cheaper -- which means that you still end up with a credit. The maximum profit is the credit received, and the max loss is the difference in strike prices minus the credit received.

OBJECTIONS:

Many traders don't hedge their naked or cash-secured put sales. Why? Because either they think it's too complicated (it's not), or they think it's not worth giving back some of the fat premium that a single put sale would generate. But what I've found is that it takes far less capital to put on a trade if it's a spread -- because of the defined risk -- and that it's easier to participate in more expensive technology stocks than an outright put sale.

SAMPLE TECH TRADES:

Comparing an outright put sale in tech giant Apple Inc (ticker symbol: AAPL) at a recent $126.83. To sell a 46day $125 PUT at today's pricing (in a moving market, obviously), would pay $3.65, or $365 minus fees. The total cost of a cash-secured put would be the $125 strike or $12,500 minus the credit received $365 equaling $12,135 before fees. (This would obviously be less on margin or portfolio margin.)

But if I really expected Apple's stock to stay flat, rise up, or go down very little between now and expiration, I could sell the same $125/115 Bull Put spread for less capital (or margin).

Sample trade:

With AAPL at $126.83
SELL-TO-OPEN (STO) the AAPL 125 PUT (46d to exp) for $365
BUY-TO-OPEN (BTO) the AAPL 115 PUT (46d) for $102
Credit received: $263 minus fees, which is the max profit

If AAPL stays flat between now and expiration, I keep the premium received. It can also drop to $125 -- or down -1.44% before my spread is tested. Obviously that is not a big buffer and could likely happen in a single or couple trading days, but if I'm neutral or bullish, I might just keep the premium. My total risk is only the difference between the strikes $10.00 (or $1000) minus the credit received $263. This means I'm putting on an AAPL put spread for $737 risk. (You can also sell $5, $2.50, and $1 wide spreads on some tech stocks (including weeklies) to reduce your overall risk.

Here's another:

If I'm bullish on content-streaming company Netflix (ticker symbol: NFLX), with a recent price of $649.55, I could earn some premium 'income' by selling a put spread and never owning the shares. With a higher volatility recently, NFLX options pay rich premium compared to some other tech stocks. This is where selling at 1 standard deviation lower (68%) makes sense. With such an expensive and volatile stock right now, a put spread -- and it's defined risk -- helps you profit but also stay out of assignment-risk if you don't want the stock put to you at $64,955 per 100 shares.

Sample trade:

With NFLX at $648.78
SELL-TO-OPEN (STO) the NFLX 545 PUT (32d to exp) for $575
BUY-TO-OPEN (BTO) the NFLX 515 PUT (32d) for $284
Credit received: $292 minus fees, which is the max profit

Obviously, the risk is $3000 minus the credit received ($292), or $2708, minus fees. The reason trades like this are interesting is that you have over 15% downside protection before your short put is tested, and that on

$2708 risk, a possible gain of $292 is over 10.78% ROR (return on risk). I encourage you to calculate your own risk, ROI, ROR, or other stats in whatever way makes sense to you. (Check the resources page for help with this!)

VARIATIONS:

The variation, especially in a neutral or soft market is to sell the put spread, and then unravel it into a sold put so that you can get into the stock. You sell a bull put credit spread, take in the credit, and as the stock goes lower into you range and below your sold put, you cash in your bought put (your hedge) and lower the cost of this stock once it's finally assigned. (Be careful though! Any time you disassemble a spread trade, your risk jumps way up!)

Let's assume I'm interested in owning 300 shares of Oracle Corporation stock (ticker symbol: ORCL), recently trading at $43.78.

Sample trade:

With ORCL at $43.78
SELL-TO-OPEN (STO) 3 of the ORCL 43.5 PUT (39d to exp) for $127
BUY-TO-OPEN (BTO) 3 of the ORCL 42 PUT (39d) for $71
Credit received: $171 minus fees, which is the max profit.

But since I think Oracle might drift lower, my plan is to wait for the price of Oracle to drop inside my spread so that I can (hopefully) make a small gain on my hedge put, and turn this into a naked or cash-secured put trade.

Now let's discuss bull call spreads on tech stocks...

7. Strategy IV

Bull Call Spreads

THE BASICS of a Bull Call Spread: Buy a call and sell a call at a higher strike price simultaneously to reduce your overall cost. The maximum profit is the distance between the two strikes minus the cost. The maximum loss is what you spent on the spread.

Buying a call in a bullish tech stock can be very expensive, so by selling a higher call to offset the cost - and cap your gains -- it becomes possible to participate in upside movement. A bull call spread is actually like a stock replacement strategy for a covered call. You own a call (it will expire, so it's different than stock), and you're selling a call against it. In this case, because you're spending money to open the trade, this is a debit spread.

OBJECTIONS:

The objections to a bull call spread are easily understood. You're buying something that can cost real money, but will still expire -- possibly worthless. And if you are right about your bullishness, the sold call -- while limiting the cost -- caps the upside.

The benefit of a defined risk is that if you are bullish, you have some direct participation in the upside potential. Since you don't have to buy the stock, the cost is much less to have one call spread than to buy 100 shares of stock.

SAMPLE TECH TRADES:

Assume that I am interested in the enterprise secure platform stock Palo Alto Networks, Inc (ticker symbol: PANW), recently trading at 176.50. If I wanted to buy 100 shares and ride it to the upside, it would cost me $17,650, plus fees (or less on margin).

Sample trade:

With PANW at $176.50

BUY-TO-OPEN (BTO) 1 PANW $175 CALL (46d to exp) for $815

SELL-TO-OPEN (STO) 1 PANW $195 CALL (46d to exp) for $135

Cost: $680 minus fees, which is the max loss

Upside potential: The difference between the strike prices here ($195-175=$20) is $2000 minus what I paid, means that max gain is $1320, on $680 risk. Max loss is obviously the full amount debited, the $680.

VARIATIONS:

Of course, it's possible that if the stock moves down right after you establish this trade, you might be able to close out the top call at a small profit. (Remember any time you take apart a spread you increase your risk.)

But if you still have lots of duration left in the calls, and you're still bullish, you can close out the hedge and make this a long call. Then, of course, your risk becomes the full cost of the long call ($815) minus any profit received from closing out the other call. If it's a news driven, marketwide sell-off, it might be possible to buy back the call and resell it at a later point to reduce your risk again.

The other thing I regularly do with these is turn them into calendar spreads by putting the two options in different months.

If I was very bullish in shares of Microchip Technology Incorporated (ticker symbol: MCHP), a semiconductor company that recently traded at $47.60, I might buy a call in an out month, but sell a call in the front month.

Sample trade:

With MCHP at $47.60
BUY-TO-OPEN (BTO) 1 MCHP $47 CALL (123d to exp) for $280
SELL-TO-OPEN (STO) 1 MCHP $49 CALL (32d to exp) for $65
Cost: $215 minus fees, which is the max loss

The hope with this trade is that the stock will rise in value, but mostly after the sold call expires in 32 days. After that, the stock MCHP has to trade above $49.15 within 123 days for me to profit, which is to the total of the $47 strike plus my initial cost ($215).

Next up let's discuss iron condors.

8. Strategy V

Iron Condors - Bull Put and Bear Call Spreads

THE BASICS: Iron Condors combine the selling of an out-of-the money bull put spread with an out-of-the-money bear call spread for a credit. The premium that you receive (minus commissions) is your maximum profit.

OBJECTIONS:

The three main objections to this trade are the complexity, the extra commissions to put on four legs, and that the losses can far outweigh the credit received. As far as complexity, this is simply two vertical spreads, and if sold far enough away from the current price of the stock, they can be an income producing vehicle. The commissions should not be a huge factor is these are meant to be sold and likely expire worthless - they won't have to be closed out. (You can also negotiate with most brokers on commission structure if you do a fair amount of volume in trades like these.) The amount that's possible to lose, compared to the credit received is manageable if you take assignment occasionally and don't try to buy-to-close a condor that goes against you.

SAMPLE TECH TRADES:

If you expect that your favorite technology stock is range bound, then selling an iron condor -- defining that range -- can be a profitable way to benefit.

Say I already own shares of digital communications products and services company Qualcomm, Inc (ticker symbol: QCOM), which recently traded at $66.62. Maybe I'd like to make some additional income from my holdings in additional to their dividend (2.90%), and some possible covered calls.

Since I notice that the stock seems range bound-- either after or before some news event, announcement, earnings, etc -- I've decided to sell an Iron Condor.

Sample trade:

With QCOM at $66.62

SELL-TO-OPEN (STO) 1 QCOM 60 PUT (46d to exp) for $45

BUY-TO-OPEN (BTO) 1 QCOM 55 PUT (46d) for $14

SELL-TO-OPEN (STO) 1 QCOM 71 CALL (46d to exp) for $70

BUY-TO-OPEN (BTO) 1 QCOM 76 CALL (46d) for $14.50

Credit received: $87 minus fees, which is the max profit.

The max loss at expiration is the width of one side of the Condor (call or put -- can't be both!), minus the credit received so $60-55=$5.00, or $500-87= $413. Personally, what I like to consider with condors is the relationship between the full loss, risk to the potential gain. On $413 risk, a gain of $87 minus fees is 21% ROR (return on risk.) Even with $15 in commissions and fees [on the high end of retail brokers], that's a potential $72 gain on $428 risk, or 16.8% ROR. But as I mentioned before, calculate your ROI-ROR any way you want, any way that makes sense to you. Some even calculate the annual return for comparison, meaning if I made this return in 46days, how would that play out if I repeated it for the entire year. (I don't always use that because it's so hard to find the same market conditions and volatility to be able to repeat a trade consistently in any open ended way. I'm sure someone can repeat trades like this every 46 days, but to my point, they're likely different underlings and different market conditions.) Your mileage may vary, as they say...

VARIATIONS:

Of course these condors can be skewed in a number of ways depending on your outlook. If you're more bearish, then you can make the call side closer to IN-THE-MONEY, or vice-versa. If you want to collect more on one side then the other you can have a wider distance between the strikes.

Here's a sample where perhaps I'm slightly more bullish on International Business Machines (ticker symbol: IBM), which recently traded at $166.20 and pays a 3.10% dividend yield. Each 'wing' of the condor is five dollars wide, but the PUTS are closer to the recent price (more IN-

THE-MONEY), and the calls are more OUT-OF-THE-MONEY to give the stock room to move a little higher.

Sample trade:

With IBM at $166.20; Iron condor, slightly more bullish
SELL-TO-OPEN (STO) 1 IBM 162.50 PUT (46d to exp) for $317
BUY-TO-OPEN (BTO) 1 IBM 157.50 PUT (46d) for $182
SELL-TO-OPEN (STO) 1 IBM 172 CALL (46d to exp) for $155
BUY-TO-OPEN (BTO) 1 IBM 180 CALL (46d) for $71.50
Credit received: $219 minus fees, which is the max profit.

Next up, let's talk about undefined risk with strangles.

9. Strategy VI

Strangles

THE BASICS: Selling a put and a call on the same underlying stock at an equal distance near or out of money is called a strangle. This is a way to take advantage of higher volatility, and sell time decay and inflated premium.

OBJECTIONS:

For most new traders, the main objection to selling strangles is the undefined risk. But if you realize that you're taking advantage of high volatility, and by extension, higher option premiums, you realize that it can be managed -- (especially by selling at or beyond 1 or 2 standard-deviation strike prices.) Selling a put on its own is widely understood as a solid way to open a new position in a stock. But selling a call alone is often considered the way to unlimited risk. But when you combine the option premiums from selling both the put and call, the extra income generated in a strangle is an added margin of error. When you realize that the stock can either go up -- towards the call side or down, toward the put side, then you realize that the expiration risk can only be one-sided.

SAMPLE TECH TRADES:

Imagine I noticed a spike in volatility and increase in premium around the IT services firm Radware Ltd (ticker symbol: RDWR). So I decide to sell a strangle at just beyond one standard deviation on the upside and the downside.

Sample trade:

With RDWR at $23.40
SELL-TO-OPEN (STO) 1 RDWR 21 PUT (32d to exp) for $30
SELL-TO-OPEN (BTO) 1 RDWR 26 CALL (32d to exp) for $40
Collect $0.70 in premiums, or $70 minus fees.

For either side to be tested, RDWR has to go down to $21.00 - $0.70 collected or $20.30 (down 13.2%!), or up to 26.00+.70 collected or $26.70 (up 14.1%) within 32 days. Since the stock is close to its 52-week high ($24.91), you might consider widening the strikes if concerned.

If you do these kinds of trades regularly, even around an event like an earnings call, you might be able to see why some traders consider strangles a consistent way to make option 'income' from their favorite volatile growth stocks.

VARIATIONS:

The simplest variation on a strangle trade is to skew it based on whether you're especially bullish or bearish. In the RDWR trade, if I was worried that the stock could run up and take out it's 52-week high, I could move up only that side of the trade, selling perhaps the $21 PUT and the $27 CALL for $56. Since that credit is very small, compared to the risk and the capital required, I might not make this trade as a strangle.

A strangle can also be the opening trade in a put sale. If I'm planning on selling a put (cash-secured or on margin) and I believe the stock will pull back, selling the strangle increases the premium received, (almost like selling a covered call on a stock you don't quite own yet!)

Sample trade:

In a soft market, perhaps I think networking and communications stock Juniper Networks (ticker symbol: JNPR), recently at $27.19, will continue to pull back. So I decide to buy 100 shares but start with a strangle to take advantage of the premiums available.

With JNPR at $27.18

SELL-TO-OPEN (STO) 1 JNPR 25 PUT (46d to exp) for $53

SELL-TO-OPEN (BTO) 1 JNPR 29 CALL (46d to exp) for $63

Collect $1.16 in premiums, or $116 minus fees.

Because I think there's a risk of the stock drifting down -8.02% to $25, a price I'd be happy to buy the stock, I'm treating the strangle like a glorified put sale. Because the total premiums (call and put) add up to $116, before fees, and then my cost basis would be $23.84 per share if exercised. Warning: if you're wrong, and you're assigned on the other side, you'll be short 100 shares of a stock that you're actually long-term bullish on, but hopefully short-term bearish enough to be able to sell and get out. (When that happens, sell a put -- it's the inverse of a covered call: long stock, sell a call, so short stock, sell a put...)

Now let me share some final thoughts...

10. Final Thoughts

Of course there are many other options trading strategies that you can use in your regular trading. These include butterflies, ratio spreads, naked calls, bear call spreads (alone), and more. This book has outlined the trades that I currently use, but I encourage you to explore the others. I honestly believe that the more you know about options trading, the more powerful the derivatives become to your trading.

On most trading platforms, you can even combine your trade ideas into a single custom trade. For example, if you decided to sell a put on a tech stock that you were very bullish on and simultaneously buy a (debit) bull call spread, then the premium received on the put can help finance the cost of the call spread.

Here's an example:

With Amazon, Inc (ticker symbol: AMZN) at $430.05, a $405 PUT with 47 days to go pays about $1025 (minus fees). If you're bullish on the stock and prepared to buy 100 shares if the put gets exercised ($40,500 or less on margin), you might combine this trade with a $430/$440 call spread on the same expiration. The $430 CALL costs $19.95, and to hedge the call you sell the $440 CALL at $15.50, making a total cost of $445, before fees. Since you took in $1025 for the bull put spread, you still have a credit of $580 after buying the call spread.

What can happen?

• If the stock stays flat or drops lower but not beyond the $405 strike, all three options would expire worthless, but you'd keep the $580 difference from above.

• If the stock goes up, you'd keep the bull put spread premium, and also make some money on the call spread depending on the move, and the time decay. Since the difference of the strike price ($440-430=$10.00) minus the premium paid ($4.45), is the max profit $555 minus fees.

• If the stock is above $440 at expiration, then your max gain is that $555 plus the $1025 collected from the put sale, or $1580.

• If it's below $405 at expiration, you'll be exercised at $40,500 minus the premium $580 credit (minus fees), or $39,920. That works out to $399.20 per share, where you will start to lose money.

• Additionally, since the put credit is big ($1025), there are other call spreads that can be fully financed here: the same $405 PUT sold can finance a $430/450 CALL spread with a $210 credit remaining, or a $432/460 CALL spread with a $20 credit, minus fees.

Lastly, don't be afraid to create watch lists and paper-trade a few of these strategies to get comfortable. Rather than risk any real money on a new options plan, write down all the market conditions, the prices of everything when you would sell (or buy), and then follow the trade all the way through until execution. (If you're interesting in a complete electronic paper trading experience, look at the last entry on the resource list in the next chapter!)

Check out these resources mentioned in this book, trade slowly, and never buy anything you don't fully understand. You're reading this because you know you need to remain a life-long learner when it comes to your investing, your personal wealth and finance, and your family's long-term financial health. That's what I've chosen. And to you, best of luck trading, investing, and growing your finances -- may you make a small fortune! :)

11. Resources List

DOUGH.COM, visual options trading software, investing portal, and finance network access of TastyTrade

FINVIZ.COM, financial visualizations (stock screeners and heat-maps)

INCREDIBLYUSEFULNOTEBOOKS.COM, makers of a trader log and investing journal, among other products

MEETUP.COM, a great way to find traders and investors in your area and meet in person

PERCENT-CHANGE.COM and PERCENTAGECALCULATOR.NET, - nice sites to calculate your gains, risk, downside protection, and more

STOCKCHARTS.COM, good simple, free charts online, with indicators - without logging into your trading accounts

STOCKTWITS.COM, Social platform for ideas, links, and
            charts for the investing community
            (Twitter-based)
STOCKTOUCH.COM, iPad heat map and screener app
TASTYTRADE.COM, an amazing free web-based financial
            education network

and

TD AMERITRADE / The 'Think or Swim' Options Broker
            -- This is the powerful stocks, options, forex,
            futures trading platform I use; I would refer
            you to this broker and trading platform
            above all others (they even have a great
            paper trading version!): http://bit.ly/
            TDameritradeOPTIONS

12. Your Opinion

If you enjoyed reading this short but hopefully HELPFUL book, it would be GREAT if you would help others find it as well. **LEND** it, **RECOMMEND** it, or **REVIEW** it.

About the Author

AUTHOR
Alan Kerrman

Alan Kerrman is an individual investor who lives near Boston, Massachusetts, USA. He is NOT a finance professional and is NOT a registered investment advisor, but an enthusiastic and motivated retail trader, investor, writer, and full-time educator. He wants to succeed with his money, and wants to help you succeed with yours by sharing what he's learned about finance and investing along the way. He lives in an old New England house with his wife and daughter. Alan Kerrman runs the site: www.dripinvestingplans.com.

Author's Note

"Writing about personal finance, stocks, trading, business, entrepreneurship, and more is a very rewarding process for me. I've been blogging and ghostwriting about a lot of this stuff for years, so it's nice to finally publish a couple short books sharing my thoughts, approach, and strategies! I continue to learn, want to always provide great value and help others, and I like to add to my growing collection of books and ebooks -- it makes my wifey and daughter proud. Thanks for reading! -- All best, A.K."

Please consider leaving a review of this book, and thank you!

Please visit:

www.dripinvestingplans.com